CW00400595

Table of C

PANTIES

Live Your Best (French Inspired) Life

JENNIFER MELVILLE

Introduction

onjour! Thank you so much for picking up this little book of mine. My guess is the title grabbed your attention because like me, you are a lover of all things French! We definitely aren't alone in our obsession. The French are known the world over for their exquisite cuisine, award-winning wines, fabulous sense of style, stunning art and architecture, passionate history and their exuberant *joie de vivre.*

I've been a Francophile for as long as I can remember, and surely before I ever heard mention of the term. As a young Canadian girl, living in a bilingual province, I was fortunate to learn French in school. I had many fabulous teachers over the years who made it their mission to inspire their students to embrace the French language and culture. I always chose France as my country of study for school projects and presentations, taking things so far as to don a beret and serve camembert to classmates! I remember the semester one of our classmates returned home after a year-long exchange program in France. She had transformed! She seemed to glide down the hallways with her flowing scarves and heady perfume trailing behind, and her lips puckered into a perfect pout. The rest of us, in our oversized sweatshirts and ripped jeans, rolled our eyes behind her back, but the truth is, I was jealous! I knew in that moment I too wanted a French makeover.

Over the course of my life, I've had the great pleasure of visiting Paris and various other regions of France a number of times. Each time I depart, I do so with a heavy heart, and a deep longing to bottle up the essence of France and bring it home in my suitcase. On my most recent trip to Paris, I set upon a mission to soak up the beauty and magic of the city with every ounce of my being. In fact, I went with no itinerary, no set plans and no must-see list of things to do. My goal was to wander aimlessly, breathe in the atmosphere, and revel in the magnificence of it all.

This book is not a guidebook to Paris, nor does it offer a behind-the-scenes peek into the secret lives of Parisians. These musings and contemplations came to me while dining in Parisian cafés and bistros, lounging in the city's parks, and meandering through its marvelous streets. They draw on my experiences travelling in France from both the distant and recent past. What started out as a personal journaling exercise, morphed into what currently sits in your hands—*Paris in my Panties*. Why my *panties* you may ask? It seems rather personal, but that is my intention. It wasn't enough to bring Paris home in my back pocket. I felt a connection with the City of Light that was intimate and sensual in nature. I was so enthralled with the sights, tastes, sounds and scents of my surroundings, that I wanted the sensation of Paris' sumptuous touch to linger on my skin.

Do you share in my deep desire to Frenchify all aspects of your life? *Paris in my Panties* offers a wide variety of suggestions on how to live an inspired life, with Paris as your muse. Grab it off the bookshelf any time you find yourself in a slump and in need of an uplifting sprinkling of Parisian magic. This book serves up a small sampling, a taste, *un goût* from the vast menu of inspirations Paris and France have to offer. Pick and choose what ideas please your palate (indulge in seconds if you so desire), and leave the rest for others if they don't suit you.

I believe that we all have a little Parisian living inside us, she may just need some gentle coaxing and encouragement to reveal herself. When I'm in a French mood, I like to imagine that I'm channeling my long lost relative, *Geneviève de Malleville.* (The surname Melville originates from several settlements in Normandy with the name *Malleville,* so I made up this fictional character for fun!) I have found that living a French inspired life elevates our experiences and fills our natural craving to invite more beauty and joy into our day-to-day lives. You can choose to adopt a Paris mindset anytime, anywhere, from the most banal of life's moments to the most extraordinary.

I'm so excited to share my delicious Parisian diary with you. (Only my best of friends are privy to these juicy details.) Let's pretend we are meeting up in a quaint little café. Go ahead and order yourself *un café et un pain au chocolat.* (I'll have *un thé au lait et un croissant, s'il vous plaît).* Are you all set to jet off to Paris with me? *Allons-y!*

1

Just Do It

There were so many reasons *not* to take this trip to Paris—stories of Covid travel headaches, the exorbitant price of the plane tickets, busy family schedules, and a small poodle with big attachment issues. These were just a few of the reservations rattling around in my head when I flirted with the idea of booking the tickets. I couldn't help but ask myself, "Is it really a *good idea* to go to Paris *right now*?"

Like most people, I haven't travelled in over two years. The last time our family ventured on a trip was March 2020. We arrived in Guadeloupe (yes, a *French* island in the eastern Caribbean), the same day our Prime Minister, Justin Trudeau, declared to all Canadians, "Let me be clear, if you are abroad, it's time for you to come home." Unable to change our flights, we hunkered down in our villa (admittedly a little lockdown paradise), and tried to make the most of our vacation. We caught the last Air Canada flight off the island ten days later.

As the two-year anniversary of the pandemic came and went, I developed an itch to travel. When I spotted a local news article that WestJet was reinstating direct flights from Halifax to a handful of European destinations, I perked up, or more accurately, I jolted into action. I pushed my feelings of trepidation and anxiety aside, and just went for it! (Note that as an accountant, I did implement one tiny cost-cutting measure to ease my financial concerns. I decided to leave the kids [and dogs] at home! A big *merci* to my dear sweet mother who volunteered to hold down the fort. I don't feel guilty, by the way. My boys told me a trip to Paris sounded "boring". That's fine, my dears, the thought of dragging you around the City of Light doesn't sound like much fun to me either.)

As Nike famously says, "Just do it!" What dream do you have whirling inside you? Maybe it's time to clear away the self-sabotaging roadblocks you set up for yourself and just go for it. Open that business, write that novel, go back to school and yes, book that trip to Paris! Keep in mind that every piece of the puzzle doesn't have to fall into place in this very instant. Regardless of your starting point, you can begin by taking small steps towards your dreams *today*. Create a business plan, write the first chapter, investigate part-time learning programs, or start squirrelling away money into a travel fund.

As our plane taxis down the runway, and I settle into my seat, I can't help but savor the delicious taste of anticipation. The magic and allure of Paris are calling my name, and I'm so glad I pushed my fears aside and chose to listen. After all, as the saying goes, "Paris is *always* a good idea!"

2

Embrace Café Culture

Utterly exhausted from our red-eye flight across the Atlantic, I've got a one-track mind when we finally reach Paris and check into our quaint boutique hotel. As much as my body wants to collapse in bed, I'm buzzing with excitement and energy, and eager to start exploring. I don't want to waste a single precious moment of the Parisian experience! Of course, my body stages its own mini French revolution against my enthusiastic plans. I decide to negotiate a compromise. My body can take a break, as long as I am happily perched front row and center in a classic Parisian café!

While it's hard to choose my *favorite* aspect of the Parisian experience, the French café culture is very near the top of my list. One of the selfish reasons I left the kids home this time around is that I wanted to soak in as much leisurely café time as possible. (We have travelled with our children to France a couple of times, and there is nothing they hate more than sitting around cafés and walking aimlessly, which happen to be two of my favorite activities. During one of our trips, I was pregnant with my first child. He still tried to ruin my vacation, and he wasn't even born yet!)

Intrigued by their legendary literary history, I check out both *Café de Flore* and *Les Deux Magots*, whose past patrons include the likes of Pablo Picasso, Jean-Paul Sartre and Earnest Hemmingway. I prefer the café scene in the early mornings, when the Parisians themselves stop in for a quick espresso and chat with a friend on their way to work. Later on in the day, the tourists take over, and the seating is a bit more cramped. I love how the tables are set up with both chairs facing the street; the perfect staging for people watching (also ranking high on my favorites list).

If you crave a more French inspired life, I highly recommend you embrace a café culture mindset. This is possible, no matter where you live! North Americans are notorious for taking their coffee to go. Instead of sipping your coffee in the car, on the bus, or at your desk, allow a few extra minutes in your schedule and actually *take a seat* at your favorite coffee shop.

If you are someone who works from home or brews your own coffee, have fun creating a café in-spired space within your living area. Since I live in the country, where my best café option is Tim Hortons, I opted for this approach. I converted my front porch into my own personal French café. I purchased an in-expensive café table for two at Ikea. It's so tiny that it could easily squeeze into almost any corner. I sur-rounded the space in bright red geraniums (a com-mon sight in Paris) and even arranged the chairs side-by-side so that they are both facing the view. While I can't do much about the lack of people watching, I can listen to the birds, watch my dogs sniff around the lawn, and enjoy our view of the ocean.

Present your refreshments as if you were being served in a French café. I decided to purchase a tea-cup from Café de Flore while I was there so I could bring an authentic piece of the Parisian café experience home with me. Although overpriced, it is worth the pleasure it brings to each and every morning. Get yourself a set of tiny espresso cups. Drink your *chocolat chaud* from a bowl. Place a couple of squares of dark chocolate on your saucer. Add special touches that will enrich the experience. Take the time to sit back and truly savor your coffee and surroundings. It is most certainly one of life's simple pleasures.

3

Develop and Air of Insouciance

I expect Paris to be more bustling and fast paced, but as my husband and I walk the streets, I feel myself relaxing and letting out a big exhale. The vibe where we have set up headquarters, Saint-Germain-des-Prés, or the sixth arrondissement, is quite chill and nonchalant (especially when you step off the grand boulevards and onto a side street). It really embodies the spirit of the French attitude of insouciance. The locals seem to get less rattled about everyday hassles like traffic, line ups and waiting for *l'addition* (the bill) at the restaurant. They appear less rushed and distracted than their North American counterparts (speaking from experience of course!) Don't get me wrong, there is a lot of activity going on in Paris. It seems to me, however, that it is the tourists that are frenzied, and not the Parisians themselves.

Soaking up the carefree atmosphere inspires me to slow down, take life less seriously, and to stop caring so much about what other people think. (Always easier said than done!) Doesn't the notion of walking through life with an air of French insouciance sound liberating? Set yourself free from unimportant worries and anxieties. You can't please everyone, and let's be honest, would you really want to anyway? Stay true to yourself, and stop fretting over what others think of you. The next time feelings of self-consciousness start to arise, put your new blasé attitude into practice and say to yourself, "Whatever! I don't really care." If you want to take it next level, you can say as the French would, *"Je m'en fou!"*

I felt apprehensive about naming this book *Paris in my Panties*. I considered going with something more conservative like *Paris in my Pocket*. In the end, however, I decided to embrace my newfound French attitude and say, "Who cares what others think?" I personally love the title and it captures perfectly how intimately I want to embrace a French inspired life. So, panties it is…and for those who are offended, *"Je m'en fou!"*

4

Learn the Language of Love

I was lucky enough to learn French growing up, even though I come from an anglophone family. Living in Canada, which is officially a bilingual country, I was able to complete my twelve years of schooling in a French immersion program. So, although my language skills are rusty, I'm holding my own here in Paris. I think I am a bit of an enigma, because the Parisians can't quite pin me down. I'm often asked where I'm from, and they are surprised to hear I'm Canadian. (Since I learned French through school, I don't have a traditional French-Canadian accent and tend to use less regional slang.)

Even though I struggle now and then to retrieve vocabulary from the dark and dusty corners of my brain, I *refuse* to allow myself to converse in English with the Parisians. I want to soak in the full French experience, and I'm on a mission to improve my French skills! When I'm stuck for a word, I simply ask for help. Despite the stereotypes about Parisians, it has been my experience that when asked directly, waiters, store clerks and even strangers on the street are happy to provide a quick, impromptu French lesson. My advice to travelers is to adopt a curious mindset. Ask questions! One of the reasons I'm attracted to travelling in France is because I speak the language. This permits me to connect with people on a deeper level and allows for a more meaningful, richer and tastier French experience.

There is a reason that French is referred to as the language of love. It has a pleasing, melodic rhythm and flow that is music to the ears. If you don't speak French, why not add a sense of romance to your life by learning the language? If you do speak a bit but your skills are a little rusty, then look for opportunities to brush up on them. It is an enriching experience to expand your mind and learn a new language, and you certainly don't have to visit a French speaking area of the world to acquire the skill. The opportunities and options for learning are endless!

Sign up for French lessons, in person or virtually. Join a Meetup group in your community to improve your conversational French. Download a language app on your phone and reach for it during downtime instead of falling prey to mindless scrolling. Watch French movies, and if you are really up for a challenge, turn off the subtitles! Read a French book with a translation app close at hand so you can improve your vocabulary and comprehension as you work your way through the text. Listen to French music and sing along to the lyrics, which are usually accessible on music apps such as iTunes. (I enjoy doing this to Carla Bruni's album *Quelqu'un m'a dit.*) Seek out *any* and *every* opportunity to practice your newfound skills!

I make a point of tuning into French radio stations while I'm chauffeuring my kids around the city. I often listen to the news, which helps expand my vocabulary and also improves my ability to chat about politics and current events (which the French love to do!) In this day and age, French stations and podcasts are easily accessible through streaming.

If you are a fellow Canadian, another fun little thing I do is make a conscious choice to read the French text on any product packaging. (Our packaging is bilingual by law.) When you aren't sure of a word, just flip over the item and check the English translation on the other side! Again, seek out any opportunity to sprinkle a dash of French romance into your everyday life.

5

Exude Confidence

While I'm bubbling with excitement over the resurrection of my French language skills, by poor husband is experiencing less than stellar success with his attempts at communicating with the Parisians. I think he's kicking himself for being such a slacker in French class growing up. Sigh… an opportunity lost! It doesn't help that we've eaten at a few Italian restaurants. (Did I mention I'm also an Italophile?) These situations are muddying the language waters to an even greater extent. Most of the text is presented in Italian, with the French translation provided below in small print. English is nowhere in sight.

Neither one of us drinks alcohol anymore, but my husband does enjoy virgin cocktails on occasion to whet his appetite. He spots an exotic sounding drink on the menu called "succo d'arancia" and is keen to try it. Our waiter, however, is extremely baffled by my husband's request for "the sugary orange-flavored virgin cocktail on the menu". I make an attempt to help by scanning the cocktail list, but finally spot what my husband is referring to on the regular drinks menu. I quickly realize his glamorous cocktail is nothing more than orange extract, in other words, orange juice!

After a few fumbles like the one I just described, my husband is definitely feeling a little gun-shy when it comes to ordering his food. He normally has a very loud, booming voice (I would suggest *too* loud), but here in Paris he's practically whispering his orders to the waiters. I realize that his issue is confidence more than skill. Most of the phrases he's using are really quite simple (e.g. *un croissant et un café s'il vous plaît*). It's apparent that a more confident mindset will produce better results. He will be easier for others to understand, and will become more self-assured in return. A win-win!

This little lesson learned in Paris can be extended to so many areas in life. There is something to be said for drawing on the "fake it till you make it" mindset.

What areas in your own life bring about feelings of insecurity? Maybe you are afraid of speaking in large crowds (I'm with you on this one!) Instead of shrinking into the background, *choose to exude confidence* (even if you are shaking in your ballet flats.) Try raising the volume of your voice, making eye contact and practicing good posture. These small adjustments in your demeanor will make you more visible. People will take notice, and listen to what you have to say. Don't we all want our voices heard in life? (Yes, even the introverts among us!)

6

Go to the Source for Style Advice

As I nibble on my morning *baguette* from my front row seat at Les Deux Magots, I'm marveling at the fashion show parading before me. I conclude that the sidewalks of Paris are in fact informal catwalks. I made sure to arrive at 8 a.m. sharp to ensure I didn't miss the highlight of the performance—everyday Parisian men and women walking their kids to school. I take notes furiously! This slice of everyday life in Paris is the essence of what I want to capture, bottle up and take home with me. I'm not so interested in the high-fashion, luxury side of Paris. I want to see how middle-aged women just like me live, dress, eat and go about their day-to-day activities. And while I can't invite myself into their homes (although I've been lucky enough to receive invitations on past trips), I can glean a great deal of insight and information just through people watching.

The first thing I notice is that Parisians come by their sense of style honestly. They start learning how to dress at a very young age, and they carry these skills with them throughout their lives. As a mother of two teens, I've done more than my fair share of people watching outside of schools back home in Canada. There is a marked difference in how French children dress across all ages. The elementary school children dress casually, but well put together. There is a noticeable absence of glitter, fairy dresses, sports logos and superhero advertising. The high school kids dress with a certain edge (usually with a cigarette in hand), but show much less skin than their North American counterparts. I've noticed at home in Canada that the sports bra is now considered a shirt. Such is *not* the case in France! (Luckily, I don't have a daughter, so I don't have to deal with this on a personal level. I'm imagining, *"Je m'en fou!"* being spat at me.)

Do you strive to carry yourself with a sense of authentic French style as I do? Although we might have some catching up to do, seeing as most of us didn't grow up with a French *maman* to show us the ropes, I believe we can learn to carry ourselves with that French mystique at any age. Yes, we old dogs can learn new tricks (and just for fun, let's pretend we are posh poodles). If you really want to learn authentically French tips and tricks, you must go to the source. You aren't going to pick up the French vibe reading North American magazines, watching North American movies, admiring mannequins at the local mall, and seeking inspiration from North American style bloggers and brands. Even those fashion sources that aim to offer "French fashion advice" feel staged and contrived in my opinion.

Seek out authentic French sources for the true French experience. I realize we can't all visit Paris for a people watching adventure, but thanks to the digital age, you can still access the experience virtually. I follow two particular *Instagram* accounts that offer a taste of pure Paris street style. Check out *@parisiensinparis* and *@paris.street.style* if you want a dose of authentic inspiration. I've also found that French films have a more real-life vibe to them, with the actresses presenting themselves in a more genuine fashion than their American counterparts. I love Marion Cotillard's character Fanny in the film *A Good Year*. Her outfits define the perfect Provençal summer wardrobe of my dreams!

7

Dial it Back

In terms of style and grace, French women have long been regarded as almost mythical in status. It's hard to pin down exactly what gives them that indefinable air of *je ne sais quoi*. In an effort to shed some light on the puzzling French woman phenomenon, I've committed to doing some serious people watching on this trip. My husband and I have made a game of it called, *"Oui ou Non"*. When a woman walks by, we take a guess on whether she is French *(oui)* or a tourist *(non)*.

As it turns out, we are pretty darn accurate with our predictions. What I've noticed is that it's more about what the French women are *not* doing, than was they *are* doing! It's about *what is missing* from the equation.

Here's a laundry list of what I generally did *not* spot on a French woman:

- Fake eyelashes (These are ubiquitous in North America. In fact, there was a time I sported my own pair of fake lashes, until I experienced a disastrous and painful allergic reaction to the adhesive. Never again!)
- Long acrylic nails, nail art or nails painted in bright colors such as yellow, orange, blue or green.
- Heavily padded push up bras (This is discussed in greater depth in chapter 9)
- Thick, heavy foundation
- Heavy, dramatic, penciled-in eyebrows
- Bleach-blond hair
- Foam flip flops
- Artificially plumped lips
- Super short jean cut-offs (bum cheeks usually on display) or heavily distressed denim
- Full sleeve tattoos (Tattoos are visible but tend to be small and much more discrete.)
- Pajama pants (another common North American favorite)

- Bedroom slippers
- Athletic clothing while *not* exercising (As a runner, I was happy to note many French women running through the parks and yes, they were certainly wearing leggings.)
- An abundance of exposed skin
- Head to toe luxury designer goods

Obviously, there were exceptions, but overall these were my observations. The "abundance of exposed skin" one was a very accurate predictor. What I noticed is that while a French woman might wear a short skirt, she'll go with something full coverage on top. Sure, her crop top might give us a peek of her belly, but she'll be sure to pair it with high waisted, wide leg trousers and a leather jacket. Many of the North American girls I spotted wore super short strapless dresses with cut outs around the mid-section (so short, in fact, they needed to wear bicycle shorts underneath to stay decent). Any more skin and they might as well have just thrown on a bikini!

What I took away from this informal study is to *dial it back.* If you too want to emit that elusive sense of *je ne sais quoi* the French are famous for, be discreet and selective in what you choose to highlight. When it comes to beauty and style, choose to embrace an *au naturel* mindset. Interestingly, even the dogs were sporting natural hairstyles! As a poodle mother and lover, I was on high poodle alert while I roamed the streets of Paris. I expected Parisian poodles to be coiffed to the nines. I was happy to learn my own dogs, Coco and Junior, are very much on trend with their disheveled hairstyles. They are basically two little Parisian pooches!

If on the other hand, there are items on the *"non"* list that make your heart sing, I suggest you refer back to chapter 3. Do what makes *you* happy and don't worry about what others think! Tap into your French insouciance. If anyone makes a comment about your tattoos or your bright teal nail polish, you can just shrug *à la française* and proudly state, *"Je m'en fou!"*

Bring the French Pharmacy Home

Another legendary aspect of the French culture is *la pharmacie*. French women are known to rely heavily on common drugstore brands to keep their skin looking fabulous, healthy and youthful.

Unfortunately, my first experience with a French pharmacy was less than pleasant. Our family was enjoying a dreamy two-week vacation in Provence when I came down with an unfortunate, uncomfortable and untimely yeast infection. *Le sigh*! It had to be dealt with if I was going to be able to enjoy the remainder of my vacation…and quickly.

Although my language skills are good, apparently our school system failed to include the term "yeast infection" in its curriculum. The closest thing I could dredge up from my brain for the word yeast was *champignon* (mushroom!) My translation app wasn't much help either because it was producing the word *mycose* (mycosis), which after I googled it, sounded more like a form of blood cancer. I decided to brave the pharmacy and do the best I could to communicate with my limited medical and anatomical vocabulary.

Pharmacies in France are much less self-serve in nature than they are in North America, so I was required to go up to the counter and explain my issue. Of course, the pharmacist was an attractive young Frenchman, and I could feel myself blushing before I even attempted to open my mouth. At the very last minute, I came up with a brilliant idea. Remember my product packaging trick from chapter 4? I quickly googled Canesten's Canadian website (the product I use at home in such an unfortunate circumstance) and just as I hoped, all their information was presented bilingually. Instead of speaking, I just pointed to my phone. After a quick scan of my screen, the pharmacist nodded, retrieved what I needed, and rang me though the cash. (For future reference, the proper translation of yeast infection is *une infection a levûre.* You never know when you might need this!)

Despite my uncomfortable introduction to the French pharmacy, I'm always sure to pop into one during my travels to pick up a dose of French beauty in a bottle. In particular, I love the product lines offered by both Avène and Nuxe. Spritzing a bit of Avène's *Eau thermal* on your face is a great way to cool off on a hot day. I sometimes use it to set my mineral makeup as well. Nuxe has a number of delicious products that smell divine. I'm a fan of their iconic *Huile prodigieuse*, a dry oil that can be used pretty much anywhere (face, body, hair, nails). It comes in a few different scents, but I'm partial to the original version with its sun-kissed aroma.

Incorporating a French beauty routine into your day-to-day is a fun and uplifting way to live a French inspired life. You are buying cosmetics anyway, so why not choose those that are fabulously French? The great news is you don't have to travel to France to access these amazing French pharmacy finds. Many of them are now available in North American stores, and for those that are not, you can order them online. I live on the outskirts of a very small Canadian city with a population of just under 450,000, and I was shocked to see that my local pharmacy carries a wide array of French brands. Another selling point is that they really aren't overly expensive! (You can pick up a bottle of Avène's cleanser *Lait démaquillant douceur* for a mere $20.)

Have fun hunting down French pharmacy alternatives to your regular beauty products and live like a true Parisian! Here's a great website to get your started on your treasure hunt: www.frenchpharmacy.com. *Bonne chance!*

9

Pass on the Padded Push Up

Although my visit to Paris isn't a shopping trip per se, I did arm myself with a list of a few "essentials" I wanted to pick up while visiting the fashion capital of the world. The French are famous for their lingerie, so my shopping list includes some pretty new undergarments. (Yes, I do intend to literally bring home *Paris in my Panties*!)

I'll admit, before I arrived, I felt a bit intimidated by the thought of walking into a French lingerie store. I've struggled in this department my entire life. Let's just say I fall outside the spectrum of normal when it comes to my bra size. (It's been officially measured at 30AAA. Yes, this size actually exists!) Shopping for bras at home in Canada has always been a nightmare, and I have been referred to the preteen section on numerous occasions. This always feels degrading and deflating as I'm a full-grown woman, not a little girl in the market for a cutesy training bra. Eventually I discovered a couple of North American designers that make custom bras for *petite* chested women like me. Traditional retail stores just never served my needs.

I've done my research before this trip, and I'm holding out hope for one particular French lingerie brand—Ysé. Here's what I pick up off their website, "…Ysé creates collections to make our bodies look glorious, without cheating or using tricks. Our lingerie: designs as beautiful and authentic to what you are. Designed by women, for all women from AA to E cup, Ysé wants you to be tender with yourself. To consider your body as a force that creates your beauty and your freedom." They sound pretty convincing, so I track down one of their sweet little boutiques in the third arrondissement.

After I shoo my husband out of the store for startling another customer trying on lingerie, I peruse the racks and squeal inside with excitement. Everything is exquisitely beautiful, and most importantly, the designs seem to celebrate the female form in its natural state.

There is a noticeable lack of the heavily padded push up varieties (which just serve as lacy voids on my body). It's hard to choose just one, but I settle on a bra called *le Triangle l'aurore,* crafted from Swiss embroidered tulle in my favorite color, blue. I also pick up a pair of matching panties. *(Bien sûr!)*

The storefront is set up like most French boutiques, which I discuss later in chapter 33. Only one item of each style is on display, so you must request your size from the salesclerk. American bra sizing differs from European, but when I explain my very *petite* size to the woman behind the counter, she doesn't bat an eye. She nods reassuringly and slips off into the back room. When she returns, she proudly presents me with something she thinks will suit just perfectly! She is not mistaken. I can't believe how well this dainty little bra fits my chest—no gaping or puckering! (It seems I have graduated from a AAA to a AA cup.) Once again, I silently squeal with excitement.

The French seem to celebrate the female body in all shapes and sizes. On Ysé's website they explain that it is imperative to be able to offer designs to their customers that don't include padding or molded cups. In order to do this, they tailor make their prototypes in each cup size; so the A cup bra is going to look a bit different to the DD bra in the same style. This allows them to ensure proper fit and support.

I'm not suggesting French women don't wear padded and push-up bras, but based on my observation, most women walking the streets embrace a more natural female silhouette. The next time you are in the market for a new bra, choose something with more French flair and with a bit less stuffing. Seek out a lacy, feminine and delicate bra that makes you feel beautiful, while still providing the support you need. Of course Ysé isn't the only brand available. I could have spent two full days shopping for lingerie, but as an accountant, I forced myself to stay on budget. They do ship to North America, so it is a viable starting point. It's worth virtually window-shopping their website for inspiration. I love that they don't airbrush away belly bulge, cellulite and stretchmarks on their models. This is just another example of the French embracing an *au naturel* mindset.

10

Become Your Own
Master Chef

To the French, cuisine is a form of art, and although we don't visit any Michelin starred establishments, we certainly do our best to savor and appreciate every bite of Parisian deliciousness that crosses our lips. The truth is, I have pretty simple tastes, so I gravitate towards foods and dishes that are unfussy. That being said, simple is *not* synonymous with plain or boring in France. I'm finding that the most basic of dishes exude a sense of elegance and sophistication that has my taste buds swooning.

Our first meal upon arrival in Paris is a late breakfast or brunch. Exhausted from the overnight flight and lack of sleep, we hit the first café we come across, just around the corner from our hotel. I order *une omelette au fromage* along with a side salad. My husband chooses the same, except he goes for *les frites* instead of the salad (and I sneak a few when he's not looking). I am amazed that something as simple as an omelet, with so few ingredients, can taste so decadent, delicious and satisfying. I suspect the chef must have sprinkled it with savory French fairy dust, because the omelets I whip up at home pale in comparison to this little work of art gracing my plate.

What this experience teaches me, is that we don't have to become (or hire) master chefs to experience the joy of French inspired cooking at home. Even the simplest of dishes can be elevated to first-class status with the help of fresh ingredients and a few learned techniques. (This is really good news for me, because my skills in the kitchen are lacking!)

Start with the freshest ingredients you can get your hands on. It's pretty difficult to create a masterpiece with substandard ingredients, especially when your recipe only calls for a handful of them. I've eaten many salads in France, and what sets them apart is the freshness and quality of the produce. A dish of fresh ripe tomatoes with a splash of vinaigrette and a dash of sea salt is heavenly, and so easy to pull together! If you can fit your local Saturday farmer's market into your schedule, take advantage of the opportunity to get your hands on freshly picked produce. Because I have busy teens in my life, Saturday mornings are not a convenient time for me to shop. If you share in my reality, look into the availability of farm-to-table delivery boxes in your area. The produce is usually harvested on delivery day, and as a bonus, you will be supporting a local business.

Embrace Leonardo da Vinci's wise words, "Simplicity is the ultimate form of sophistication." Choose *just one simple dish* to master and perfect. Designate it your *pièce de résistance*, the highlight of your culinary repertoire and the signature dish you are known for. Watch videos to pick up tips and tricks from the experts. Experiment with your ingredients until you get them just right. Infuse your efforts with love, passion and attention to detail. My husband has set his sights on mastering the omelet, while I'll be handling dessert. Pana cotta has been my Paris indulgence, so I think it needs to take center stage in my life back home.

(Yes, I realize panna cotta is an Italian specialty, but the French, not surprisingly, do it very well!) What will be your signature dish?

11

Practice Good Manners

Parisians may have a notorious reputation for being rude, but this is *not* my experience. In fact, I'm impressed by how polite, formal, kind, generous and open they are. I've visited France numerous times, and I can only think of one instance where I was regarded with complete disdain. Admittedly, I deserved it.

Eighteen years ago, my husband and I decided to book a last-minute trip to France. We had just found out I was pregnant, and viewed this getaway as a final hurrah before the responsibilities of parenthood monopolized our lives. We combined our two passions (I'm a Francophile, and he's a surfer), and settled on the French surfing destination of Guéthary. Guéthary is located near Biarritz, on the south west coast of France, which is about a seven-hour car drive from Paris. I still question our sanity when booking our flights. (I blame it on first trimester brain fog.) Instead of choosing a logical flight path through Biarritz or Bordeaux, we flew straight into Paris. It wouldn't have been that bad, if we weren't carting around an overstuffed, eight-foot surfboard bag. As two accountants, looking for any opportunity to save a euro, we chose to hitch a ride on the metro into downtown Paris instead of catching a cab. Yup, that's right, we stuffed ourselves, our luggage and those ridiculous surfboards on the Paris metro at the height of rush hour. As you can probably imagine, we were the target of many dirty looks, head shaking, sighs and a few choice words I won't repeat here. This black cloud of distain followed us to the hotel, the car rental agency and beyond! I can only look back now and think how idiotic we looked!

This time around, I've packed a light and *petite* suitcase, and it's been smooth sailing. In fact, I almost feel like I'm being given the royal treatment. The French seem to take their greetings *very seriously,* and are much more formal than North Americans. I could really get used to being politely greeted with, *"Bonjour Madame!"* instead of the typical, "Hey" I get back home in

Canada. This touch of formality seems to elevate day-to-day moments from mundane to extraordinary.

I do wonder where their reputation for rudeness comes from, because my experience here has been so pleasant. I realize I'm dealing with people in the service industry (hotels, shops, restaurants), but the stereotypical French waiter falls into this category, so something feels amiss. I may be wrong, but I believe some people are looking for reasons to call the French rude, just to keep the myth going and perpetuate some kind of twisted fantasy. I experience it firsthand while ordering myself a crêpe in a bistro. I ask the waiter how the eggs are prepared, but he doesn't know the English word for "sunny side up". A kind French woman in the next table over chimes in to explain. The North American woman sitting on the other side of me leans over and whispers loudly, "Can you believe how rude he was to you? I just give it back to them!" I was dumbfounded, as he hadn't been rude at all! (I suspect if this is her attitude, she encounters rudeness everywhere she goes.)

I've also heard complaints that the Parisians will refuse to converse in French with you, even when you are trying to speak French yourself. Here's my take on it. They are very keen on customer service, and they seem very proud of the fact that they speak English so well. (Their lightly accented English is music to my ears. I decide they speak English better than I do!) They switch to English as a courtesy, to offer you the best possible service. Even though I speak French, my husband does not. I believe they are speaking English to "us" in an effort to make him feel included in the conversation. Second, the restaurants and cafés are bustling. Speaking English is probably just easier, faster and more efficient for them.

What can we learn from this? Assume that people are acting with good intentions and stop looking for rudeness or nastiness. You'll feel lighter and more happy when you don't feel like the rest of the world is working against you. I'm also really taken with the importance the French place on proper greetings and salutations. I plan to do my own little part when I return home and make the extra effort to hand out cheerful greetings…I might even throw in a *bonjour* here and there to spice things up!

12

Find Yourself Un Boyfriend

I don't pretend to be a fashionista. I dress to please myself and tend to focus on styles, cuts and colors that best suit my figure and complexion. I'm not one to follow fashion week, or read the latest issue of Vogue. This means that I'm not always up to date on the latest and greatest trends, which suits me just fine. That being said, there is one obvious trend on the streets of Paris that I simply can't ignore—*le boyfriend*. No, I'm not referring to a boy toy dangling from the arms of French women, but rather a classic, straight-cut, oversized boyfriend blazer. *Le boyfriend* is so ubiquitous, I would suggest it doesn't classify as a trend, and is really just considered a wardrobe staple. I see it worn by young and old, over jeans, over dresses, glammed up, or dressed down. It comes in a rainbow of colors, but I prefer those in a classic menswear wool. My husband and I naturally add it to our repertoire of *I Spy* games, which now includes: *Oui ou Non, Poodle Alert* and *Le Boyfriend.*

As I mentioned in chapter 9, this vacation was never intended to be a shopping trip. I did, however, arm myself with a short list before I arrived, which includes lingerie, a new pair of white sneakers to replace my worn-out pair, and a handful of beauty products from *la pharmacie.* (Oh, and a hefty serving of *macarons* for the kids, to soften my feelings of guilt for leaving them behind.) In an uncharacteristically spontaneous move, I promote *le boyfriend* to the top of the list! Since my goal here is to bottle up the essence of Paris to pack in my suitcase (or panties), *le boyfriend* suddenly turns into an essential that I can't go home without.

As it turns out, it's not as easy to find the perfect *boyfriend* as I had hoped. (I guess this is true of the human variety as well!) I visit several stores and try out many different versions. The cut and the length are key factors that you have to get just right. The goal is to capture an oversized look, without losing yourself in the jacket, and my 5'3" frame is presenting a challenge. I finally settle on "the one", which is *le Jacques* blazer by Rouje. (My husband was shocked they didn't offer one named after him—*le Todd*. Clearly *le boyfriend* needs to have a French ring to it.) Since we are in the spring/summer season, I go with a cream colored one in a cotton/linen blend. I pay full price, but now that I know my size, brand and style, I add a wool version to my fall/winter wish list. I plan to pick it up second-hand and at a much lower price. (Buying duplicates of current wardrobe pieces is something I discuss in my book *Preloved Chic*. If saving money interests you, I encourage you to check it out.)

If you want to dress like a true Parisian, consider adding *le boyfriend* to your list of wardrobe staples. It's far from a frivolous purchase because it is such a versatile item. It's one of those pieces that doesn't have to match perfectly with everything you're wearing. For the most part, the women I observed were sporting it as a coat or jacket. They threw it over everything and anything, and they instantly looked stylish and incredibly chic (with a dash of insouciance).

There are tons of reviews online for the various brands that offer *le boyfriend,* so if you are interested, I encourage you to start there. Try to find a reviewer that has a similar body type to yours. I was specifically looking for a blazer that would work on a shorter person. Maybe you need one that suits your large bust, or tiny shoulders. Again, the cut and length are crucially important. I tried on a few blazers that tapered too much at the waist, and *le boyfriend* vibe was completely lost. I also tried on an amazing grey wool blazer at APC, but it didn't quite cover my bum cheeks.

I assure you, *le boyfriend parfait* is out there waiting for you, it just might take some digging to find him.

13

Become Une Flâneuse

*D*o you know what *une flâneuse* is? The closest English equivalent would be a loiterer (female in this case, the masculine version being *un flâneur*). The word loitering in the English language definitely has negative connotations associated with it. We most often see it used near mall entrances where "no loitering" is permitted, and violators are threatened with prosecution. The French approach loitering from a different perspective, one that actually reveres and encourages lounging, dawdling, hanging out, meandering, sauntering and wandering aimlessly. (I do need to point out that one French/English translation site I stumbled on offered the term *poodling around* as the equivalent of *flâner*. Of course, as a poodle mom, I'm latching on to this one for future use.)

I arrive in France with the primary goal to *flâne* (or poodle around) as much as possible. This is the number one thing my children despise doing (even more than sitting in a café once the *pains au chocolat* have been devoured), and without them tagging long, the city of Paris is my oyster!

Our favorite place to *flâne* is le jardin du Luxembourg, located a short fifteen-minute walk from our hotel. We make a point of sauntering through this greenspace every day of our trip to soak in the beauty (there are works of art hiding behind every shrub), people watch, seek out shade, rest our tired legs, savor our ice cream cones, close our eyes, and play pretend Parisian. To be honest, this entire trip focuses on the fine art of doing nothing. I'm not ashamed to admit that we haven't visited any museums or galleries. I'll save those for my next holiday. My goal right now is to let my legs carry me wherever my heart desires, and soak up as much Paris as possible!

When was the last time you went for an aimless stroll through your own community? I have to admit, I don't do this very often myself. I walk my dogs around our neighborhood loop for exercise, but I rarely venture on a sightseeing stroll through the historic part of my hometown. (It's literally been years.) This really is a shame, because we have a beautiful waterfront in the city of Halifax, and the opportunity to *flâne* is staring me in the face.

Pencil yourself in for some poodling around! (Just don't do it outside the mall.) Go for a walk with no particular destination in mind. Saunter along at a slow pace and soak in the sights. Take a moment to stop and sit on a park bench, and treat yourself to an ice cream while you are at it.

14

Plant Red Geraniums

The first time I visited Europe, I was the tender age of nineteen. I had signed up for a summer work abroad program in France with one of my girlfriends from university. Although our planned destination was France (we actually ended up working in Greece), we first landed in Amsterdam to spend a few days sightseeing before hoping on a train to Paris. I remember being completely mesmerized by Amsterdam's overflowing flower markets and in particular, the dazzling array of fresh tulips that seemed to come in every color imaginable.

Parisians also love their flowers! I often spot them toting large bouquets of roses and peonies on their way home from work (and yes, quaintly tucked into the baskets of their bicycles). If I had to choose one flower that captures my heart in Paris, the simple red geranium wins the prize! I swoon at the sight of the quintessential Parisian building façades, their wrought iron grates adorned with overflowing window boxes of bright, cheerful geraniums. It's a view that is simple, classic and incredibly chic!

While you might not be able to replicate that classic Haussmann-style architecture at home, you can certainly skip off to your local garden center and treat yourself to some classic Parisian inspired red geraniums. If your window configurations are suited for it, go the extra step and install a few window boxes.

Back home in Canada, one of my first outings upon returning from Paris is a trip to the nursery. While I normally enjoy choosing a wide variety of colorful potting plants, this time I filled my cart with geraniums and nothing else. My house isn't conducive to window boxes, so I planted mine in terra cotta pots and created an attractive display on my front porch. I enjoy tending to my little plants each morning with my cup of tea, watering, deadheading and soaking in their uplifting and sunny disposition. My grandmother actually kept geraniums in her home year-round as house plants, so I plan to invite this little taste of Paris indoors come fall.

15

Dress to Impress Yourself

I hate to harp on clichés, but they often exist for a reason! One cliché I'm finding to be truthful is that the everyday Parisian is a better dresser than your average North American. In my view, the word "better" does not necessarily refer to dressing up, or dressing more formally (although there is some of that!) It's more about dressing with intention, and making an effort to look good for the personal pleasure of it.

As I people watch from a front row seat at Café de Flore, I can't help but admire the variety, creativity and self-expression on display. It seems anything goes—from well-cut suits, to flowy bohemian ensembles, to classic trench coats, to jeans and t-shirts, to colorful tailored pants, to pretty sundresses, to *le boyfriend*. Actually, that should be rephrased to say, anything goes, *with the exception of* sloppy sweats and head-to-toe Lululemon. The only people decked out in athletic wear are the runners, and yes, they are actually *running*!

The impression I get is that people are dressing for the fun of it. They are creating outfits that make them feel good and that bring an extra dose of beauty and joy to everyday life. Again, that doesn't necessarily translate to dressing formally or dressing up. It might mean wearing a pair of jeans and a t-shirt, but with a few extra touches thrown in to elevate the look from plain Jane to stylish. It's also apparent that *fit matters.* I doubt everyone has a personal tailor, but the Parisians seem to make a point of wearing clothes that look sharp and *fit their bodies perfectly.*

Do you find yourself in a style rut? Are you dressing on autopilot every morning, reaching for whatever is easy, comfortable and hopefully clean? Do you dress for the sole purpose of clothing your body? I've been there! (In fact, I wrote an entire book about my personal style journey called *Elevate Your Personal Style: Inspiration for the Everyday Woman.*) Maybe it's time to up your game and seek inspiration from the French

approach to dressing. If all this sounds rather super-
ficial to you, and you are skeptical that your wardrobe
choices can actually impact your moods and self-esteem,
I challenge you to commit to one week of intentional
dressing. Reassess your opinion when the seven days
are up! I suspect you may never look back.

Push past the urge to pull on the easy-peasy black
leggings or the crumpled jeans and t-shirt lying on the
floor. Walk into your closet and pick something nice
to wear; something that makes you feel good on the
outside *and* the inside. You can achieve an elevated
look, even if you want to keep things casual. Choose
a pair of jeans that are freshly washed and hanging in
your closet—the ones that give your butt an extra lift
and make you feel fabulous! Take a pass on the faded
old t-shirt and choose your brilliant white V-neck with
the flattering neckline. Instead of pulling your hair
back in a messy bun, sweep it up into a ponytail tied
with a pretty silk scarf. Take a few extra seconds (yes,
literally seconds) to pop on a pair of earrings, a neck-
lace and a belt. Instead of your running shoes or flip
flops, slip your feet into a chic little pair of leather flats.

When it comes to dressing *à la française,* it's all about those *petite* details that are carefully and consciously added to an outfit. While they might appear insignificant at first glance, the little extras can have a huge impact on how pulled together you look, and more importantly, how pulled together you *feel.*

Again, dressing well is not about trying to impress other people. It's a form of self-love and self-care. *It's all about you!* While packing for this trip, I spent far too much time, effort and mental energy trying to configure the perfect Paris wardrobe. Now that I'm here, I realize that the Parisians seem to place great importance on relaxed self-expression. There is so much variety walking the streets, I quickly realize no one is giving me a second glance! The only person concerned with what I'm wearing is me.

Most people are too concerned with themselves to worry about or notice what you are wearing (unless of course I'm around taking style notes, then yes, you are being watched). Dress to impress yourself and infuse your life with more fun, positivity and happiness!

16

Celebrate Your Inner Goddess

Our hotel is a two-minute walk to the Louvre and the adjacent jardin du Carrousel and jardin des Tuileries. We enjoy strolling the grounds of this area in the evenings, when the museum has closed its doors for the night, and the bustling crowds have dispersed. It's the perfect place to *flâne* or poodle around. I'm particularly attracted to the interesting statues on display, and always stop to take a moment to read the accompanying plaques for an impromptu lesson in art history.

I don't proclaim to be a sophisticated art aficionado, with a great deal of insight to offer, but I can't help but notice that these sculptures of the female form don't necessarily adhere to our modern-day vision of the perfect body. I don't see any washboard abs, perfectly rounded breasts, perky bum cheeks, or model thin legs. In fact, most of the women I observe showcase rounded bellies, healthy thighs, soft curves and reasonably sized breasts. They appear *normal,* realistic achievable…and *beautiful.* Interestingly, their bodies were considered to be the ideal for that period in time. If you'd like a clear image of what I'm referring to, do a quick internet search on *Trois nymphes* by Aristide Maillol. These ladies do not look like the figures gracing today's catwalks and magazine covers!

At what point in history did things get so twisted, that we women have been conditioned to place unrealistic expectations on ourselves? When did the definition of the ideal body enter the zone of impossibility for the vast majority of us? I'm not going to pretend I have this whole body image thing figured out, but spending time in the company of these goddesses has helped shift my perspective.

Instead of filling your brain with unrealistic images, seek inspiration from true, authentic and healthy sources. You don't have to visit Paris in person to get in touch with *your* inner goddess. Browse through

photos of ancient art, or tune into body positive so-
cial media platforms. Celebrate your muffin top, baby
belly and menopot. Recognize that if you had been
born a few hundred years earlier, you could have been
a model for some of the great artists. Walk the runway
of life confidently with self-love in your heart with
your head held high!

17

Dine Mindfully

I t's a particularly warm afternoon in Paris (finally!), which means I'm in the mood for *une glace* (an ice cream) to cool off. My husband and I spot a little ice cream shop not far from le jardin du Luxembourg, one of our favorite hangouts. You probably won't be surprised to learn that the ice cream is served in the shape of a flower. This is *Paris* after all! Could I expect anything less? After choosing my two *parfums* (which of course sounds more lovely than the word flavor), I watch the gelato artist create the prettiest little ice cream cone I've ever laid eyes on.

Sadly, there isn't much time to admire her work of art, because it is melting at a fast and furious rate. As we make our way over to the gardens, I try to keep up with the rivulets of chocolate and black cherry running down my hand. Unfortunately, by the time we locate a park bench, my ice cream is gone! I feel cheated and disappointed. I was too busy walking to appreciate the rich flavors and dreamy creaminess of my treat. I resist the urge to buy another cone from the vendor in the park, just so I can relive the experience more mindfully.

I notice a stark difference between the way Parisians and North Americans approach mealtime (or snack time, referred to as *le goûter* in French). There is a much greater focus on enjoying your food in France, by taking the time to sit down and be fully present for the experience. In North America, there is a grab and go culture, which is really what fast food is all about! I have a vivid memory from one of our trips to Provence that really drives home this point. It was a Sunday afternoon, and we were wandering around the quaint town of l'Ile-sur-la-Sorgue. The parks were bustling with families enjoying a weekend picnic in the fresh air. I noted that they were *not* stuffing their faces with Subway sandwiches. (On a side note, I was shocked to see this franchise operating in Paris, as I can't imagine choosing to eat their bread over a French *baguette.* As an accountant, I'd like to get a peek at their financial statements to see how they are really doing!) The French were picnicking in style, with many of the comforts of home, including cutlery, ceramic dinnerware, cloth napkins and wine glasses. Yes, the French even take a humble picnic to the next level!

One of my most poignant observations of this phenomenon was the sight of a homeless man sleeping on a park bench in Paris. In addition to his clothing and blankets, he had a very tidy and organized set of plastic containers piled up next to him. They were filled with all his mealtime essentials including salt and pepper, mustard, herbs and spices, and a full set of flatware. The scene broke my heart, but I do hope these comforts of a home kitchen serve to elevate his mealtimes and bring a sense of pleasure to his days.

We could all probably use a reminder to slow down and tune in to the experience of mealtimes and the enjoyment they provide. View your food as a source of pleasure and not just a source of fuel. Sit down to eat, whether it's a four-course meal, or a light afternoon snack. (Please avoid your desk at all cost.) Put away your phone and focus your attention on the food and the company. Even if you are just having a quick *café*, sip and savor it. Instead of grabbing a coffee to go and gulping it down on the commute, enjoy it on the spot at the coffee shop. If that's not possible, save it until you get to the office and take a seat in the lunchroom. This will give you an opportunity to catch up with coworkers before the hectic day begins.

This is something I definitely need to work on myself. Family mealtimes are fairly structured, but when I'm home alone during the day, I find myself grabbing snacks on the go while passing through the kitchen. They usually disappear before I have a chance to taste them. "Take a seat" is my new mealtime motto… are you with me?

18

Pick a Color, Any Color

I was always under the impression that for the most part, Parisians dressed from head to toe in black. As a result, I packed a *petite* capsule wardrobe consisting of black, black and more black (with the exception of my classic beige trench.) As it turns out, I'm the most somber looking person walking these cobblestone streets.

It may have something to do with the fact that I'm visiting in the springtime, when most humans are craving relief from the heavy darkness of winter, but the Parisians I've observed (and believe me, I'm giving everyone a thorough looking over), are proudly and confidently sporting garments from every color of the rainbow. And it's not just a pop of color here or there in the form of a scarf, handbag or fantastic pair of shoes. I'm seeing spirited and bold use of color everywhere, in both men and women.

In fact, it's the fashion sense of the French men that has stolen my heart and captivated my imagination. Red pants appear to be the "it" item at the moment. I might more accurately describe the color as reddish orange. I've decided to grant it a proper name and refer to it as "Roussillon", after the region in the south of France that is famous for its red ochre earth. (Crayola, this would make a great name for a crayon color!) I like to imagine that these stylish Parisian men wear their daring red pants to remind themselves of carefree summer holidays in the south. I suggest my husband pick up a pair in one of the boutiques, but he's not convinced he could pull them off at the office. (Accountants aren't known for taking fashion risks!)

It seems the women have chosen a different "it" color, which I would describe as Kelly green. I've never seen more green pants in my life (with the exception of perhaps a St. Paddy's Day celebration). Interestingly, I just did a quick *Google* search and this color pops up on Pantone's Fall 2021/22 color trend report. They refer to it as Leprechaun (Pantone 18-6022). I guess the Parisians are proudly still wearing it even though we've moved on a to a new season.

Don't fall prey to the misconception that you need to dress in dark colors if you want to exude a chic Parisian vibe. I assure you, Parisians are indeed embracing color, and so should you! In fact, I believe that color is one of life's simplest, yet most delicious pleasures. Enveloping your body in a really fabulous color can boost your mood and put a spring in your step. Pick your favorite color and wear it with both joy and fearlessness!

I returned home from vacation feeling inspired to incorporate more color into my wardrobe. Admittedly, when I opened my closet door, I was faced with a sea of blue, black and white staring back at me. It took some digging, but I eventually found a vibrant fuchsia scarf that I've owned for years but have never worn. I decide to take the baby step approach with the color experiment, and vow to wear this bright little scarf with confidence. Maybe someday I'll even pick up a pair of "Roussillon" pants of my own!

19

Embrace les Arts

As our taxi weaves its way towards our hotel, I catch my first glimpse of some of Paris' most iconic sights (*l'Arc de triomphe, le Dôme des invalides, le musée du Louvre, la tour Eiffel*). I'm left speechless by the arresting grandeur and beauty of it all. (Ok, I may have just squealed.)

Although I don't make it through the doors of the Louvre this time around, I'm not suffering from a lack of exposure to the fine arts. (I do have a number of galleries and museums on my agenda for a future visit, but right now I'm too busy eating and poodling, and didn't want the experience to feel rushed.) There is art of some form hiding behind every corner, and tucked into every nook and cranny. The city of Paris itself is one giant museum and art gallery!

Creative expression seems to be infused into *everything* the French do. Window shopping (or *lèche vitrines*, which translates to window licking) is the equivalent of taking a gallery tour, free of charge. Even though many of the shops and boutiques are out of my league and price range, I always take a moment to stop and admire the stunning and fashionable displays. Each meal I order is exquisite in its presentation. I can't help but become one of those people who pulls out her phone at the table to capture a memory of the masterpiece before it is devoured.

When I return home to Canada, one of the aspects of Paris I miss the most is the constant presence of art in my line of vision. (Although I am thankful my rural life allows me to be surrounded by Mother Nature's creations. I really shouldn't complain.) I endeavor to immerse myself in more artistic experiences at home. I'm ashamed to admit I've only visited our provincial gallery once, and I did so with two toddlers in tow, so you can imagine the speed at which I sailed through it!

Set a date in your calendar to visit one of your local galleries or museums. If you can, buy an advance ticket online as a way to force yourself to follow through on your plans. Purchase a ticket to a live theatre or musical performance. Again, financially committing to a ticket often gives us the nudge we need to get out of the house. Take a stroll through your downtown area where the tourists frequent, and take your photo next to a piece of public art on display.

You can also immerse yourself in the work of great French artists from the comfort of your home. I highly recommend the film, *Water Lilies of Monet: The Magic of Water and Light.* I rented it on *Apple TV* one rainy Sunday afternoon (which offered the perfect watery backdrop), and after learning more about Monet's life and approach to creativity, I fell in love with his works. Someday I plan to visit *le musée de l'Orangerie* in Paris to view his *Nymphéas (Water Lilies)* murals up close and in person, but for now this little film quenches my thirst.

You can also choose to add your own artistic touch to everything you do! In the absence of art, create your own. This could mean signing up for a watercolor class, in person or online. It could also mean dressing with flair and intention, as we chatted about in chapter 15. Maybe you will be inspired to plate your food more attractively, with a sprig of fresh herbs on the side. Perhaps you'll take a few extra seconds when snapping a photo on your phone to consider the composition and lighting. The possibilities for expression are endless.

20

Hop on Your Bicycle

We walk *everywhere* in Paris. I hesitate to say it, but we may be overdoing it. The fact that I have to pop an ibuprofen at the end of each day is probably a sign I should back off and seek out an alternative form of transportation. I'm tempted to try out their bicycle sharing system, *Vélib',* but I'm not confident enough in my ability to navigate the traffic. The bike lanes are bustling and busy in Paris. The common sight of people texting while cycling concerns me. I decide to take a pass on pedaling, and opt to just sit back and admire the Parisians as they zoom past me on their *vélos.*

Yes, there is much to admire, because as you would expect, the Parisians cycle in style. Again, it seems anything goes, from handsome men in sharp fitted suits, to women sporting *le boyfriend* while balancing a baguette and smart phone. (I still haven't figured out how they don't show up for work drenched in sweat…or maybe they do. No doubt they just glow.) Of course, the only thing I don't spot is proper cycling attire!

All these cyclists have me inspired to dust off my own bicycle, pump up its tires and get it back on the road after a long cold Canadian winter. I've done more than my fair share of cycling in the past. (In 1996 my father and I cycled across Canada as a summer adventure. Yup, that's over six thousand kilometers!) Despite my love of the sport, I don't do it nearly enough. I commit to hoping on my bike at least three times a week from now until the snow flies in November. I do, however, refuse to give up my comfy, padded lycra shorts.

Do you own a bicycle? Is it gathering dust in the basement or garage? Maybe it's time to give it some action. I think it's one of those activities that has the power to transport you back to your childhood. If you are intimidated by traffic as I am, locate bicycle trails in your community. If you don't own a bicycle, rent one for a day. Pack a picnic (Parisian style of course) and enjoy the wind in your hair and the sense of freedom that cycling offers.

21

Live a Romantic Life

Paris is known for being the most romantic city on earth. Admittedly, it's the main reason I've chosen it as my destination. This is the first time in over seventeen years that my husband and I have escaped together, *sans enfants* (without the kids!) It's turning out to be a thousand times better than our honeymoon twenty-two years ago. I think it relates to the fact that back in our early days as a couple, we took alone time for granted. Since having kids, it's been a lot harder to carve out time for our relationship.

Don't get me wrong, family life is wonderful and rewarding, but I wouldn't describe it as particularly romantic. One of our sons is actually a werewolf, and for the first twelve years of his life, he transformed into a grouchy, screaming little monster at the stroke of midnight. The only sure-fire method to reverse this spell was for me to crawl in bed with him. I played musical beds for many, many years, often not even knowing where I was or who I was with when the sun rose.

While walking the streets of Paris with my husband (not to be confused with *mon boyfriend*), I feel free and giddy, swept up by the mystique and romance that surrounds me. I flip the kids a selfie of "Mommy and Daddy in front of the Eiffel Tower" and my seventeen-year-old son texts back, "Wow! You look so happy!" I have to admit, I *am* really happy, and it's not just because I'm in Paris. It's because I'm on vacation from my Mom role, and tapping into the *girlfriend* side of my persona. My husband and I finally have a chance to connect with each other, free from interruption and distraction, which feels decadent and seductive!

I know firsthand how hard it is to find alone time with your partner when you are chest high in raising a family. Most of the time you are just trying to keep your head above water, and at the end of a busy day with the kids, there is little time or energy left for yourself, let alone the two of you. It's something I didn't prioritize enough when my children were younger, and I can look back now and see how it led to a sense of burnout. Motherhood fills you to the brim, but at the same time, it also sucks you dry (in a very literal sense if you are breastfeeding.)

You don't need to go on an expensive getaway to make time for your relationship, although if you can swing it logistically and financially, then book those tickets, and do so guilt-free. On a more realistic level, seek out snippets of time when you can connect as a couple, and when the kids are nowhere in sight. If you both work outside the home, skip the boring business lunch and book a date with your lover. Enjoy a romantic midday dining experience at a quaint little bistro. Arrange it so that you both book a vacation day *on a school or daycare day.* Send the kidlets off to school and turn your full day into a date. How nice would it be to spend an entire day at home together, enjoying the peace and quiet, and actually being able to have a meaningful conversation?

Find a babysitter! If you are lucky, you might even have family members who will be more than happy to spend time with your sweet children, free of charge. I can't thank my dear mother enough for playing fairy grandmother while we were away. I think she actually enjoyed looking after my boys. She loves to cook, and they love to eat, so it was a winning combination.

Carving out couple's time is also about setting boundaries with the kids. We've always had an open-door policy in our house, but now that the boys are teens, I feel like we need more privacy. We've decided our bedroom should really serve as our own private space, so I just ordered a "Please Do Not Disturb" sign off Amazon (and in the spirit of adding French flair to my life, I got the French version which states, *Prière de ne pas déranger*).

You can also welcome more romance into your life even if you are flying solo. Living a romantic life is really more about mindset than anything else. Allow yourself to be inspired by the romance of Paris, and look for ways to infuse it intimately into your daily life. (Yes, right next to your skin…in your panties!) Spritz yourself in a soft feminine perfume, wear exquisite lingerie, read epic romance novels, indulge in chick flicks, burn candles, play French café music in the car, take a luxurious bubble bath, fill your home with fresh flowers, wear a pretty scarf, sleep in silky pajamas, immerse yourself in your passions, savor decadent food, let your imagination run wild…do what makes you feel divine!

22

Follow Your Nose

As a self-proclaimed country mouse, I usually associate big cities with the smell of exhaust fumes and other unidentifiable funk. I realize I'm probably viewing Paris through the lens of rose-colored glasses, (or in this case, a rose-colored face mask), but there is definitely a pleasing aroma blowing in the wind. (Yes, I get the odd whiff of urine, but there's no need to harp on that here!) The scent of perfume combined with the soft, tender fragrance of flowering spring plants is intoxicating. Yes, the clichés surrounding the French and their obsession with perfume have been confirmed.

When we arrive at our hotel, my nose picks up a distinct scent. I don't think twice about it, until the next time I waltz through the doors to the lobby and am greeted by the same scent again. I assume the concierge is wearing cologne, until I spot a few bottles of room spray for sale by the front desk. It turns out our little boutique hotel, with its twenty-four rooms, has its very own signature scent! (If you watched *Emily in Paris*, you might remember the episode where Emily pitches the idea for Maison Lavaux to create a signature scent for the newly opening Zimmer hotel.)

Gliding through the cosmetics department of Le Bon Marché Rive Gauche, (a high-end department store), I gladly accept perfume samples from every chic salesclerk who offers them. I can't pass up the opportunity to smell something pretty! As I stuff the stack of scented cards into my handbag, I start to worry their molecules might rub off on the stash of Café de Flore sugar cubes I've got hiding in there. (I feel a little bit like my late grandmother stuffing airline cutlery in her purse.)

Of all the samples I collect, I'm drawn to one called *Jardin de l'Orangerie* by Dries Van Noten. It is a light, sweet, sunny floral scent that would be great for summer. Although I'm not in the market for a new perfume

(My current daily wear is *Vanori* by Sylvaine Delacourte), I take my sample cards home to use as bookmarks. (If you read my book *Elevate Your Life at Home*, this is an example of sprinkling your home with fairy dust. I like hiding little treasures between the pages of my favorite books, to be discovered and enjoyed at a later date.)

I realize many people have sensitivities and allergies to scents. I'm actually quite picky myself, and steer clear of scented detergents and cleaning products in our home. (I also never wear scented products in public spaces that forbid them such as healthcare settings.) I've found I prefer to stick with perfumes that are subtle and discreet. This is one of the reasons I like Sylvaine Delacourte, as their focus is on incorporating clean, natural, raw materials into their fragrances.

Enveloping yourself in a beautiful scent welcomes more joy and pleasure into your life. If you have an existing collection of perfume, take those few extra seconds each day to spritz yourself with a dose of happiness. If you haven't tried perfume, but the thought of it intrigues you, set yourself on a journey to explore the wonderful world of fragrance. Admittedly, it can be very overwhelming. I started my signature scent journey by first identifying fragrances I'm naturally drawn to—rose and vanilla. From there I did a bit of internet research to narrow my search and identify perfumes that incorporated these notes. Before committing to a big bottle, you really need to get your hands on a sample and try it out for several days.

There are lots of ways to add scent to your life without committing to perfume. Scented candles, essential oils, bath and shower gels, body lotions, scented drawer liners, potpourri and of course, fresh flowers! And if you love French films as much as I do, settle in for a movie night with *Les Parfums* starring Emmanuelle Devos and Grégory Magne. It's touching, comical, and interesting and will most certainly inspire you to indulge in perfume more often.

The key point I'm making is that our sense of smell is a powerful source of pleasure, so why not indulge in some fragrant goodness, just for the joy of it?

23

Wear Cut-Offs à la Française

I t seems apparent that the French don't mind borrowing from other cultures. They know a good thing when they see it. Such is the case with blue jeans. Although they were invented in the US, they are obviously a staple in the Parisian wardrobe.

This is great news for me, since it's the only thing I've been wearing since arriving in the fashion capital of the world. Reality isn't living up to the optimistic weather forecast I obsessed over before my departure. (Does it ever?) I realize I'm Canadian, and should be tougher than I am, but I'm freezing my buns (or *brioches*) off most of the time. I'm forced to wear the same outfit on repeat—black jeans, my trench coat, and a scarf, of course. My chic skirts and dresses never even make it out of the suitcase.

Since I'm on self-assigned *style watch*, I make a point of scrutinizing and dissecting the denim choices of the Parisians I encounter on the street. I make two main observations. No surprise, wider-leg cuts are more popular. Most of us probably heard reports that the skinny jean craze has cooled off, and it appears to be fact, not fiction. This is unfortunate news for skinny jean lovers like me. Of course, since I've adopted the *dress to impress yourself* mindset, I'll still be wearing mine. That being said, I did recently experiment with a straighter-cut silhouette, and am loving it.

My next observation comes to light from the *"Oui ou Non"* game my husband and I have been playing from chapter 7. If you remember, super short jean cut-offs and heavily distressed denim are both on the *"non"* list. Let's be realistic, one of the most fabulous things about denim is how it wears. That lived-in look is highly coveted. What I *do* see the Parisians wearing, is a much more discreet version of the cut-off. A common sighting is a rough-cut hem on full-length jeans. This subtle detail adds an edgy vibe, without overdoing it. It also offers a casual touch to the lighter washes of summer denim.

I had a pair of light-wash preloved jeans that were in queue to go to the tailor. (At 5'3" most of my pants need to be shortened.) Inspired by my recent trip, I decided to take a do-it-yourself approach and chop the hems off myself. Do you have a pair of jeans sitting in your closet that you never wear, or that are just a tad too long? If you're up for it, grab a pair of sharp scissors and a measuring tape and make yourself a pair of Parisian cuts-offs. The hardest part is making sure the length matches on both legs. I suggest you cut with a conservative mindset. If they are still too long, you can always go back for a second round with the scissors. Once the hems are cut, run your jeans through the wash a couple of times to get that authentic frayed look. Easy peasy, and oh so stylish!

24

Go the Extra Mile (or Kilomètre)

A number of years ago our family visited the Provence region in the south of France. We chose to stay at an Airbnb that boasted lots of space for the kids to run around, as well as a spacious kitchen area where we could take part in some of our own cooking. (This place actually had two kitchens, an indoor one *and* an outdoor one.) We lucked out, and ended up with a very friendly, animated and talkative host who was just as entertaining to be around as the sights and events we took in during our vacation. He was a real character, and one of the highlights of our trip!

Straight from the pages of Peter Mayle's, *A Year in Provence*, Arnaud ticked the boxes on a number of French clichés. He spoke with grand gestures, he made regular use of heavy sighs and he was intensely *passionate and particular about food!* He had very strong opinions on what we should eat during our visit, and *exactly* where we should buy it. There was only one *boulangerie* recommended for *baguette*, which was a couple of towns away. On the way there, we should stop at this butcher for sausage, but a different butcher for steak, and yet another establishment for organ meats. (I didn't have the heart to tell him we were vegetarian... which came back to bite me in a very big way. Stay tuned!) The tastiest and juiciest melons *must* be purchased from the fruit stand in town on the *left* side of the street. Of course, there was only one camembert worth eating, which he crowned as *le Roi du Fromage* (aka King of Cheese). Grocery shopping was certainly not viewed as a one-stop operation as it is in North America. Making the extra effort, and driving the extra 25-50 kilometers was viewed as not just normal, but *nécessaire.*

We did our best to keep up with Arnaud's shopping itinerary, but to be honest, we did have other sights to visit and villages to explore! I couldn't justify passing up on Pont du Gard or a day in Arles to retrace

Van Gogh's steps in order to hunt down the evening meal. Somehow, I survived eating the "wrong" *baguette*, although I did have to admit, the melons he recommended were absolutely divine.

Food is one of life's greatest pleasures. The better the quality, the happier your taste buds will be and the happier you will *feel*. It's pretty obvious the restaurants where we dine in Paris are going the extra *kilomètre* to source the freshest and highest quality ingredients. Everything tastes exquisite! The notion of putting in the extra time and effort is also evidenced by the Parisians patiently waiting in line for their treat of choice at their favorite *pâtisserie*.

There is no need to take this concept to the extreme. Pick and choose your priorities and seek out those specialty items that are truly worth the extra bit of time, effort and money. Make a list of all your favorite foods and investigate the best options available in your local area.

My mom has placed corn on the cob near the top of her list. Although she lives in a rural area with half a dozen farm markets within a one-kilometer radius, she refuses to settle on anything but the best. She travels twelve kilometers to get her hands on the finest corn money can buy; the cream of the crop. The farmer sells it directly from the field! Making a trip to a farm market, or taking part in a farm-to-table delivery service (as I mentioned in chapter 10), is a great way to access fresh produce. As a salad and veggie lover, fresh greens and tomatoes are probably the two highest priority items on my list.

Olive oil and balsamic vinegar are also incredibly important to me, especially since they top the majority of my salads. We have a specialty olive oil store in town that is worth visiting, but I use the grocery store variety for cooking.

You might be surprised to find many high quality, French specialty products hiding on the shelves of your regular, giant chain grocery store. I was actually shocked to discover Arnaud's *Roi du Fromage* on display in the deli case at the supermarket I frequent. To think it had been hiding there all along! (It's called *le Rustique* if you are interested.) While I am trying to keep my grocery orders within budget, I do pick up the odd specialty item here and there. Just last week I purchased a container of *Fleur de sel le Saunier de Carmargue* to sprinkle a little dash of France on my food. Have fun treasure hunting the shelves of your own supermarket to see what surprises await you!

25

Find Your Voice

A trip to Paris wouldn't be complete without a visit to *la tour Eiffel*! We decide to make a day of it, and walk from our hotel in the sixth arrondissement to the neighboring seventh. We stop for lunch in a tiny bistro with a perfect view of the iconic tower. Although I've visited the Eiffel Tower on previous trips to Paris, the sight of its stately grandeur sends shivers down my spine. I feel as though I'm living in a dream and I'm acting out the starring role of a movie— the movie of my fabulous Parisian life!

I'm suddenly snapped out of my reverie by the sound of a blaring megaphone. It turns out there is a demonstration taking place about thirty feet from our charming sidewalk bistro. Apparently, we've chosen to dine right across the street from the *Ministère des solidarités et de la santé* (the offices of the Minister of Health). The demonstration has been organized by a large group of passionate healthcare workers who are voicing their concerns over strenuous and exhausting working conditions, which have been exacerbated by the Covid pandemic.

I have to admit, I'm not one bit disappointed that we are in for a loud and lively lunch break. The whole scene is so entertaining, and so quintessentially French, that I can't help but giggle with excitement inside. I feel lucky to be a spectator of the scene, and even find myself discreetly chanting along with the megaphone between bites!

The French are known for their penchant to protest and to make their voices heard. As an introvert, and a naturally shy person, speaking my mind is something I sometimes struggle with. While this is a great trait for avoiding confrontation, it has gotten me into trouble on many occasions.

I got our entire family in a huge predicament when I failed to admit to our food-obsessed Airbnb host Arnaud that we were vegetarians. He invited our family over for dinner one evening and sure enough, the menu consisted of meat, meat and more meat (and then more on top of that!) He served up a teetering tower of chicken, lamb, beef, pork, veal, three types of pâté, four varieties of sausage, and various unidentified organs (aka mystery meat). I discretely leaned over to my husband and whispered, "You are going to have to take one for the team Honey." I nibbled on a small bite of chicken (it was all I could stomach) and indulged heavily in the casserole of roasted vegetables his wife had prepared. My husband was pretty much forced to try everything, with Arnaud hovering over him, ready to offer seconds, thirds, fourths and fifths. I have to hand it to my boys. They adopted an adventurous mindset and dove right in. I'm pretty sure it was all for the purpose of telling schoolyard stories of all the gross and strange things they ate in France.

Living a French inspired life means speaking your truth, and doing so unapologetically. Offer your perspective, voice your opinions, speak your mind…and own it! I'm finding the older I get, the easier it is to adopt this mindset. I know what it's like to be shy, and how uncomfortable it can feel to put yourself out there. I'm definitely someone who prefers to fly under the radar. That being said, there are times when standing up for yourself is critical. My advice comes down to the old saying, "Practice makes perfect." The more you practice standing up for yourself, the more comfortable you will feel with your voice, and the less you will care what others think.

Start with something easy and non-threatening. When was the last time you lied to a waiter at a restaurant, claiming the food what great, when in fact it was terrible? The next time you encounter this type of situation, let them know you were disappointed. My guess is the kitchen would appreciate the honest feedback. My husband is really great at being assertive, which usually means situations turn out in his favor. When our flight back home to Paris was cancelled, and we had to stay an extra night at our hotel, their initial quote was double what we had paid for the previous nights. With a few carefully chosen words (in English), my husband negotiated the price down by almost half! Tap into your inner French girl and let your voice be heard!

26

Become a Creature
of the Night

I don't know if it is possible for the early bird and the night owl to coexist, but I'm doing my best to keep them both alive and well during my time in Paris. Back home, I'm naturally an early riser, up with the birds (sometimes before) at 5 a.m. I relish the quiet solitude that mornings offer, and treasure this *me time* where my schedule is clear to do as I please, whether it is to exercise, write, read or sip tea quietly while watching the sun rise. Mornings are truly magical.

The downside to greeting the day at such an early hour is that I wind down (or more accurately crash) in the evenings at a very rapid pace. By 8 p.m. I'm usually snuggling into my pajamas, with lights out an hour later. This tendency to hit the sack early most often follows me on vacation. I'm suddenly reminded of a family trip to Disney World. (Two words sum it up for me—*never again.*) After a hot trying day of braving long lines, maneuvering a mammoth double stroller and stuffing my children with overpriced, mouse-shaped ice cream treats, I'd had more than my fill of the "Magic Kingdom". I overheard someone say, "The fireworks should be starting any minute." I locked eyes with my husband and mouthed, "We need to get the hell out of here right now." I knew this was our opportunity to bolt, and avoid the post fireworks traffic jam that I anticipated. Yes, my kids missed the fireworks, but as the saying goes, "Ignorance is bliss." They had no idea they were missing out, and I got to collapse in bed at a reasonable hour.

With all that being said, I sense a shift in my internal clock while in Paris. I don't want these dreamy days to end, and so I stretch them out as long as possible, and well past my bedtime. Every evening we make our way across the Seine to the Right Bank, and amble through the grounds of the Louvre and le jardin des Tuileries. The evening light casts a glow on the intricately detailed sculptures and building façades. The effect is quite simply, *enchanting*.

Although I'll never give up my early bird ways, Paris has opened my mind to the notion of occasionally staying up past bedtime and becoming a creature of the night. If you are a parent as I am, I know you are exhausted, especially if you have very young children. It's so much easier to flop on the couch and zone out on Saturday night than it is to rally the energy and enthusiasm to go out. *I get it.* But since we are trying to live a more Paris inspired life here, I'm going to recommend that now and then you make the extra effort to get out at night and live a little. (I sound like such a party pooper, but surely I can't be the only person who needs to be dragged out of the house in the evenings, kicking and screaming. Right?)

If you struggle with attending activities that stretch into the evening, set yourself up for success. Here are a few strategies I've relied on to help me catch a second wind late in the day:

- Plan a late midday nap if you can sneak it in. Even closing your eyes for fifteen to twenty minutes can be enough to fill your craving for sleep.

- Pick an event or activity that feels easy and where you will be physically comfortable. I get so tired standing around chatting, so cocktail-style parties aren't my favorite thing to do. In these instances I usually try to find a spot to sit down. Concerts, theatre performances, films or sit-down dinners are great options as they get you off your feet!

- Go easy on the alcohol. Drinking too much is only going to make you feel more tired, plus the effects can carry over into the next day. I no longer drink alcohol, but I still have vivid memories of what it feels like to be hungover. I quit drinking when I was twenty-three because I was tired of wasting my weekend mornings feeling sick and tired! Even one drink hits me in all the wrong places.

- Go easy on the food. Overindulging on a big meal can also leave you feeling sleepy. If I'm heading out for an evening, I stick to a light dinner. This allows me more room to nibble on the treats that are usually offered at special events.

- Engage in a bit of physical activity late in the day. A brisk walk around the neighborhood can work wonders in giving you the second wind you need to make it through the evening.

- When all else fails, caffeinate! If you want to stretch your evening a little longer, have that espresso after dessert!

It's worth noting that I completely crashed when I returned home from Paris. The early mornings, late nights and jet lag caught up with me. I have no regrets though! I think the key is striking a balance.

27

Buy Your Man a Scarf

hile Parisian women remain the primary subjects of my unofficial style study, I do admit to a wandering eye. As I mentioned in chapter 18, French men are generally more adventurous with their fashion choices than their North American counterparts, and I can't help but admire their bravery. Although French women are known for their creative and skilled scarf tying abilities, I'm also impressed with the male version of accessorizing going on. *French men wear scarves*, and they do so with a sense of daring yet elegant style.

My husband has been bitten by the style bug, and while in Paris he is boldly sporting a scarf everywhere we go (the one and only scarf he owns). His scarf is surely having the time of his life, as up until this point, he has led a rather lonesome and solitary life. "Scarfy", as I have affectionately named him, has spent the majority of his days collecting dust in a dark and lonely closet...the poor guy. I imagine he is soaking in the sights of Paris and delighting in greeting other scarves on the street. I hope my husband hasn't gotten his hopes up, and vow to encourage him let Scarfy out more once we return home to Canada. I can't blame my husband, he has tried in the past to up his fashion game, only to fall victim to mockery and taunting at the office. He has taken some serious heat for wearing the same scarf that seems to blend in so nicely on the streets of Paris.

I remind my husband that it was not long ago that he was on the giving end of snide looks and comments. We have one *very* stylish man who lives in our community (let's call him Mr. GQ), and yes, he wears scarves. We once went out to dinner with a group of friends and bumped into Mr. GQ and his wife dining at the same restaurant. Mr. GQ was sporting a scarf that was draped elegantly around his neck. All the men in our group immediately started snickering over his style choice. It's worth noting that not one of thcm was dressed particularly well. I secretly and quietly admired Mr. GQ, and I suspect most of the women in our group did as well!

Are you up for a fun challenge? Buy a man in your life a scarf, and *dare him to wear it*. Give the gift of French style to your husband, son, boyfriend, father, uncle, brother, cousin, co-worker or friend. Any male will do. Teach him the phrase, *"Je m'en fou!"* so he has a quick and clever comeback line when the teasing begins!

I haven't seen our little friend Scarfy since we arrived home, but I have faith my husband might push through his insecurities and make an effort to accessorize a little more often. He was also inspired by the Parisian attitude towards style, so perhaps Mr. GQ will soon have some competition in the community.

28

Indulge

"*Je voudrais un chocolat viennois, un croissant et des tartines beurrées avec de la confiture, s'il vous plaît.*" While I normally pride myself on my healthy eating habits, my *petit déjeuner* this morning ticks *none* of the boxes on Canada's Food Guide. My selection consists of a decadent hot chocolate (so rich with cream it has coagulated), a flaky calorific pastry and sliced baguette laden with butter and jam. Despite its life-threatening fat and refined sugar content, and the obvious absence of fiber (although the jam *might* classify as a serving of fruit), I feel nourished, satiated and perhaps even a little giddy. Maybe I'm just drunk on the pure *pleasure* this meal provides! Paris, and all its enticing temptations, is teaching me to relax, loosen up, color outside the lines and *indulge* (at least on occasion).

If you read my book, *Elevate Your Health*, you know that I am very passionate about fitness and nutrition. I live a clean lifestyle that involves lots of fresh air, exercise and a primarily plant-based diet overflowing with fruits and vegetables. As I creep my way into my late forties, my goal is to age with vitality and grace, and I believe strongly that my healthy lifestyle is going to increase my chances of success. That being said, I believe there is room for *indulgence* in a healthy lifestyle. I might even argue that indulgence is a *key component* of a healthy lifestyle!

When you permit yourself the occasional treat, you keep your cravings in check, and are more likely to stay on the path of healthy living. My guess is that as soon as we classify something as forbidden, we desire it all the more. It comes down to the classic human tendency to want what we can't have. When faced with the forbidden, we suddenly develop a sense of scarcity, and so the binge begins. Ironically, we rarely enjoy these binge sessions. In our frantic state, our tastebuds become numb, and all we are left with in the end is a sore belly and damaged pride.

French women are known for their slender physiques, which I aptly observed during my time in Paris. It's no wonder the book *French Women Don't Get Fat* by Mireille Guiliano is a bestseller. Adopting a French inspired way of eating is about enjoying a fresh, healthy diet, while still allowing yourself to indulge in the most decadent fare. The focus is on *indulging with intention* and savoring every delicious bite when you do. So instead of mindlessly scarfing down a bag of chips while watching TV, serve yourself a reasonably sized, satisfyingly salty bowl. Enjoy every crunch! My treat of choice these days is panna cotta. As I mentioned in chapter 10, I've been experimenting with mastering this dish. I won't be serving it every evening, but it makes a perfect weekend treat.

Indulgences aren't just found in the kitchen, or behind the display case at a *pâtisserie*. They come in many forms—a spritz of expensive perfume, a luxurious set of sheets, warm fluffy towels, a leisurely breakfast in bed, a long and unhurried bubble bath, an aromatic bouquet of red roses and an extra few minutes to linger (or *flâne*). Choose to indulge in life's most delicious pleasures more often! What decadent indulgence do you crave the most? Succumb to those cravings and enjoy!

29

Wear White Kicks

We've all heard the advice from fashionistas and travel gurus alike, "If you want to fit in while travelling in Europe, don't wear sneakers!" It's evident to me that this guidance is outdated, as sneakers are definitely the "it" shoe on the streets of Paris this spring. That being said, one does have to be careful when selecting the *style and color* of this casual footwear favorite. An updated version of this advice should actually state, "Don't wear running or hiking shoes… as in ones you would actually run in or use trekking up a mountain." It appears many tourists didn't get the memo (the original or the revised version).

I'm thankful I packed a cute pair of white sneakers for this trip. They've been a key component of my Parisian wardrobe for two reasons. First, I fit right in!

Everyone is wearing cool white sneakers—the young, the old, and those in between. They are paired with everything from jeans to dresses. I would say the most popular brand is Adidas, but I also spot a lot of Converse. I'm wearing the French brand Veja, which also seems to be a favorite. Second, they are the most appropriate choice for walking, which the city of Paris is obviously designed for! I did pack a couple of pairs of leather flats (gold and nude), but I've only worn them on short evening walks.

It is possible to be both stylish *and* comfortable! Get yourself a cute pair of fashionable white sneakers (or *baskets* as they are called in French) and hit the streets! Save your technical footwear for the gym and the trails. My eighty-year-old mother just invested in an awesome pair of Veja sneakers herself. She went with the style called *Esplar Leather White Platine.* I love the combination of classic white with a touch of luxe platinum. *Très chic!*

30

Brush Up on French History

I've always been nostalgic, and a lover old things. As a young girl, I spent much of my childhood with my nose in a book, travelling back in time to visit friends from days gone by. (I was besties with Laura Ingalls and Anne of Green Gables.) Of course, the word *old* in a relative term. When you live in Canada, the late 19th century feels likes eons ago. One gains a whole new perspective when visiting Europe. Suddenly Anne Shirley seems like a hip and modern girl!

I'm blown away by the overwhelming sense of history on display in Paris. The remnants and reminders of a very long and complicated past come to life through every sculpture, every cobblestone, and every architectural marvel. I feel drenched in wonder. I'm so awestruck, my chest actually aches!

I find myself overcome with a burning curiosity and the desire to dig deeper. I'm constantly stopping in my tracks to google every miscellaneous artifact I stumble across (big or small). I feel an unquenchable thirst for knowledge, and I silently scold myself for not picking up more history electives in university. I've decided that while I wait for my son the young inventor to build a time machine in his basement workshop, I will immerse myself in a self-study program when I return home to Canada. My first reading assignment is *How Paris Became Paris: The Invention of the Modern City* by Joan E. DeJean.

Hit the books and brush up on your knowledge of French history. Not only is it great exercise for your brain, it will also help you acquire a deeper appreciation and understanding of the French way of life. There are a zillion topics to choose from, so start with an area of interest. You might decide to read up on the history of fine cheeses, wine making, 15th century art, the Napoleonic Wars, or the life of Coco Chanel!

I'm only a couple of chapters into my new bedtime story, but the more I get to know Paris, the more deeply I fall in love. My mind is filled with beautiful images of grand palaces and boulevards before drifting off to sleep. This provides great content for fabulous dreaming. It's safe to say we will never run out of reading material, as France's history dates back to prehistoric times. Pick a century, any century and enjoy the magical experience of time travel.

31

Wear French Fashion Brands

As a Francophile, achieving the French woman aesthetic has been on my list of style goals for years. What I have come to conclude is this: if you want to dress like a French woman, *then dress like a French woman.* The easiest way to do this is to shop as she does, by choosing the same brands and styles she fills her wardrobe with!

I'm in my glory in Paris, as all the fabulous French brands I love are on full display! I'm actually not referring to many of the iconic luxury brands you might be thinking of, such as Chanel, Dior or Yves St. Laurent. The line ups outside these shops snake down the sidewalks, and I'm not interested in wasting my precious time in Paris. To be honest, these high-end brands sit well outside my price range, and my personal taste.

I'm a fan of several of the lower and more reasonably priced brands such as Des Petits Hauts, Sézane, Rouje, Sandro, Vanessa Bruno, Maje, and Soeur, just to name a few! OK, so the term *reasonably priced* is relative. They still carry hefty price tags, but don't worry. If you've got your heart set on welcoming more authentically French pieces into your wardrobe, then I've got some great money-saving techniques to offer!

It's also worth mentioning that most of the everyday French women I observed were *not* dressed from head to heel in designer goods. I did note there was a lot of high/low mixing going on. Many of them did in fact carry a designer handbag (usually a black, discreetly logoed crossbody), which was offset by reasonably priced clothing. The only people I observed that were literally *dripping wet* in designer goods were tourists! (Usually snapping selfies in front of the fashion houses.)

I mentioned this trip to Paris was never intended to be a shopping trip. I came home with one fresh pair of white sneakers, my perfectly fitting bra and panties, and of course, my dreamy *boyfriend.* That doesn't mean

I didn't spend a fair amount of time in fitting rooms though. In fact, I tried a lot of clothes on in Paris, but instead of adding them to my shopping basket, I added them to my wish list! I may be a die-hard Francophile, but I'm also an accountant, and a girl who likes to save money.

Second-hand shopping is my secret style weapon. It allows me to fill my closet with all those fabulous French brands I love so dearly, for a fraction of the retail price. I viewed my trips to the dressing room in Paris as a research project. I made sure to record all the pertinent details of the items I tried on in my style journal (brand, size, colorway, style name). I plan to hunt them down on the used market at a later date. I've had my best luck online shopping through platforms based in France such as Vide Dressing and Vestiaire Collective. (Good news, they ship all over the world.) What better way to dress like a French girl than to dig through her closet and scoop up her hand-me-downs? It's kind of like having a cool French older sister! As I mentioned in chapter 12, I wrote an entire book on this subject, so be sure to add *Preloved Chic* to your reading list!

If you aren't familiar with French brands, then start with the list I have provided and go from there. You don't need to travel to Europe to access many of these brands. If you live in or near a large urban center (I don't), many of the big departments stores like Nordstrom carry them. You may choose to pay full retail price, or go the preloved route as I do. You can pop in, browse, try a few pieces on, and build a fantastic French wish list in the process. For those of you who reside in more rural areas, the internet is a fabulous tool. I use the size charts and online reviews all the time to gather information on pieces I'm eyeing.

Again, if your goal is to dress in a French manner, you can't go wrong with choosing authentically French style!

32

Escape

*P*aris may be a big bustling city, but there is no shortage of places to seek solitude, peace and tranquility. After finally tracking down my perfect *boyfriend* at Le Bon Marché Rive Gauche (you never know where you might bump into the love of your life), I'm ready for a change of scenery. The incessant hum of the department store has me craving quiet!

Le jardin du Luxembourg is a short walk away, so it's the obvious choice for a midday getaway. Lured by the pleasing sound of trickling water, we settle into a pair of classic Parisian park chairs next to *la fontaine Médicis*. I could sit here all day. I'm soon lulled into a reverie by the dappled light, the melodic gurgling of the fountain and the intoxicating scent of honeysuckle.

The Parisians seem to love their parks as much as I do, and the perimeter of the fountain is lined with people of all ages. The mother and daughter duo sitting next to me have brought their watercolors, and are engrossed in capturing this glorious scene on paper. The elderly couple across the water sit side by side in silence, holding hands. Two twenty-something lovers sit face to face, staring into each other's eyes with the same look of longing as the sculpted couple that adorns the fountain. A sharply dressed man in a suit munches on his sandwich—the classic French *jambon-beurre* (ham and butter on a baguette).

Escape seems to be the primary goal of park dwellers. Despite being busy places, Parisian parks somehow manage to retain an atmosphere of tranquility and calm. They strike a perfect balance between lively interaction and respite. For those in the mood for some action, one can partake in a game of *pétanque* (also knowns as *boules*), try their hand at tennis, sit down for a friendly game of chess, delight in children sailing toy boats, or join the groups of sunbathers on the carefully manicured lawns. (Park management posts signs to indicate which areas are in use, and which patches of grass are taking a rest. Everyone seems very respectful of these instructions.) For those craving some alone time, it's not difficult to secure a secluded bench, or nestle a chair into a quiet corner beneath a statue. There is something for everyone!

We all need the opportunity to escape from the hustle and bustle of our daily lives. So many of us forget to take breaks throughout the day. We hit the ground running first thing in the morning, and then collapse in a heap at the end of the day. It's no wonder many of us are so tired all the time!

Give yourself time each day to recharge your batteries. Find a place that will allow you to both physically and mentally escape. The lunch hour is a perfect time to do this. Instead of eating lunch at your desk, opt for a change of scenery. If you are fortunate enough to work near a park, take your packed lunch with you and settle onto a bench.

If you work from home, it can be difficult to separate work from homelife. Force yourself to escape the home office *and* the housework! Weather permitting, I recommend taking your break outdoors. Lately

I have been enjoying my lunch hour in the homemade café space I mentioned in chapter 2. It sits under a covered porch, so I can even settle in there when it is raining. (A good rainstorm actually gives is a cozy, hygge kind of vibe.)

I also think that bathrooms serve as great retreats, though they are usually more suitable for the end of the day. Lock the door, light a candle, put on some soothing music, pull out the bubble bath and pretend you are in a posh Parisian spa, receiving the royal treatment you deserve!

33

Practice Discernment

$\mathcal{P}$aris is a master of contradiction. While it offers an overabundance of art, fashion, food, wine and pretty much anything your heart desires, it clearly holds the opinion that "less is more". Somehow, the Parisians embrace *both* lavishness and restraint with paradoxical perfection. These two ends of the spectrum coexist in perfect harmony.

I'm a minimalist at heart, so I'm instinctively drawn to the less is more mindset on display. It is particularly evident when I walk through the doors of some of my favorite boutiques. The ambiance in these shops is airy, serene, uncluttered and spacious. A single item of each style hangs eloquently from the rack. If you'd like to try a garment on, you must ask the salesclerk for assistance in fetching your size. This gallery-like atmosphere promotes an attitude of discernment. Each piece is displayed and celebrated as though it is a work of art, meant to be admired, instead of frantically stuffed into your shopping bag. There is so much room to breathe, think and ponder your purchase decisions carefully.

This is in stark contrast to what I am used to back home in Canada, where shops are overflowing with merchandise. Jam packed racks seem to sag under the weight of their occupants. It's overwhelming to sort through the items on display and make well thought out purchase decisions amongst all the clutter, confusion and distraction. Shops at home definitely convey a "more is more" attitude. It's exhausting.

If I had to choose one word frequently used by fashion YouTubers that I *despise* the most, it would be the term *haul*. (e.g. Check out my huge ZARA haul!) Sadly, it accurately sums up the North American attitude towards consumption. The term haul is really quite fitting, because my guess is in most cases, all this stuff will soon need to be *hauled* to the landfill!

What would you rather bring into your life, a truck-load of junk, or a few high quality, carefully selected objects? It's time to ditch the greedy mindset and lean into a more French inspired way of living. Be selective with what you bring into your life. Choose quality over quantity. Own fewer, nicer things. Practice discernment in all areas of your life, and you will surely feel a greater sense of contentment, peace and ironically... abundance!

34

Plan Ahead

After spending the morning exploring le Marais district, or the third arrondissement, we plot a route back to headquarters in the sixth that will take us through l'Île de la Cité. I'm keen to catch an up close view of Notre Dame, and despite the fact she is currently undoing some major reconstructive surgery, she is the picture of beauty, elegance and grace. Once again, I am awestruck by the grandeur and magnificence before me. Just to add to the emotional ambiance, a young, brilliant violinist is serenading the crowd with *Comptine d'un autre été,* a tune from one of my favorite French movies, *Amélie.* I admit to shedding a tear.

What fascinates me the most about Notre Dame, and really *all* of Paris' monumental sights, is the tremendous amount of planning that must have gone into creating these colossal masterpieces. The intricacy, symmetry, complexity, harmony, perfection on display…it boggles the mind. Some of these treasures took centuries to construct! I wonder if today's modern technology will speed up the process of restoring Notre Dame from the ravaging fire of 2019. My husband and I spot what looks to be a temporary six story apartment complex assembled for construction workers nearby, fashioned out of shipping containers. Obviously, they are planning on sticking around for a while!

Paris, and all its glory, didn't just come to be by chance or coincidence. The French are master planners. Although we tend to associate Paris with fantasy, creativity, freedom and spontaneity, I think planning tops the list. All this is comforting news to me, an accountant and lover of balance, order, structure and schedules. It turns out my analytical calculative nature might just come in handy!

We can all learn from the French propensity to plan. Living a French inspired life doesn't just happen! You have to consciously make an effort to live with more intention. It really comes down to making a *choice* to embrace more beauty and joy into your life, and then *purposefully acting* in ways that follow through on your plans. The great news is that much of this is within your control! You can map out a way of living that incorporates as many of the little French inspired tips this book serves up as you'd like.

In my first book, *Elevate the Everyday*, I introduce the concept of the dreamy/practical list. This is basically your standard daily to-do list, with a twist. The idea behind it is to *schedule* fun and dreamy activities to ensure they happen. This might mean booking yourself for a stroll through the nearby park over your lunch hour to admire the spring blooms. It might mean allocating two hours on Sunday afternoon to work on your knitting project. Maybe it means setting the alarm clock fifteen minutes early so you have more time to dress beautifully, blow dry your hair and apply a touch of light makeup.

Again, you get to decide what your best French inspired life looks like, and then plan accordingly. I think the French would approve!

35

Break Good Bread

*I*t is my last morning in Paris, so I grab the opportunity to pop into the little *boulangerie* down the street from our hotel. This is my final bread run and my last chance to pack a taste of Paris in my suitcase. I order *six demi baguettes et deux pains au chocolat.* They will serve to Frenchify tomorrow's *petit déjeuner* and hopefully soothe the sting or returning to reality. When I inform the woman behind the counter that these goodies are on their way to Canada, she takes extra care to box them up securely to ensure they reach their final destination in one piece. I make sure to tell her she is *très, très gentille!*

My advice on this one is pretty simple and straightforward— seek out good bread. This is one of those instances where going the extra *kilomètre* is worth it. I have a friend whose husband is an airline pilot, and he regularly brings home bread from his travels. She is gluten-free, so finding tasty bread is particularly challenging. I think she really appreciates his extra efforts. Obviously we can't all go to such extremes to source our bread, but I believe it's worth taking a detour to your local bakery to get your hands on quality bread. Maybe you are lucky enough to have a French bakery nearby, run by an authentic French *boulanger* or *boulangère*!

We have a really nice bakery about a fifteen-minute drive from our home. I certainly can't make it there daily, but I do try to stop in when I'm out running errands. I usually buy a few loaves at a time and freeze the excess. Although frozen bread doesn't compare to a loaf that is fresh out of the oven, it runs a close second. My mom taught me a trick she uses to revive a day-old or defrosted loaf. She runs the loaf briefly under water then sticks it in the oven for a few minutes until it is dry and crusty. It really does work magic. So don't be shy to fill up that breadbasket!

36

Level Up

Fifteen minutes before our airport taxi is due to pick us up, I get a call. Our flight home has been cancelled! To make matters worse, the fabulous direct flight that enticed me to book the trip in the first place is no longer an option. Instead of flying direct from Paris to Nova Scotia, we now leave tomorrow with a connection in Toronto. This means our travel time has increased from six hours to a much more unpleasant fourteen.

My irritation and frustration soften, however, when I realize two things. First, this means we get a full extra day in Paris (at a heavily discounted rate, I might add, because our airline now owes us compensation.) Second, we will now be hitching a ride home on Air France, instead of the low budget Canadian airline we booked with. I've always dreamed of flying Air France, and let's just say, they did not disappoint!

Air France's approach to their safety video only serves to bolster my opinion that the French *do everything better!* Even the most banal and boring aspects of life are infused with a touch of magic, charm and an air of *je ne sais quoi*. Before we go any further, please take a moment to head over to Air France's YouTube channel and search up "new safety instructions". I'll have a *café* while I wait for you to finish…

Ooh la la, isn't it *fantastique?* I must admit, I've watched it numerous times since I returned from my trip to Paris. It transforms an incredibly boring and mundane subject into something captivating, entertaining, artistic and just plain fun. I consider it a cinematic work of art, worthy of an Oscar. (Surely it qualifies for nomination under one of the short film categories.)

Draw on this French approach to living and choose to *level up!* Add that special extra touch to anything and everything that you do. If you are plating a meal, do so with aesthetics in mind, carefully arranging the food in a pleasing manner instead of plopping it mindlessly on a plate. When getting dressed for the day, add the finishing touches that transform an outfit from fine to incredible! Accessories are your secret weapon on this one. Create an inspiring playlist of your favorite French tunes, and play it loudly on your regular morning commute. Turn the whole concept of levelling up into a game. Make *level up* your new motto and challenge yourself to implement it in everything that you do. How could you *level up* brushing your teeth? How could you *level up* your morning walk? How could you *level up* scrubbing the floors? Ask yourself, "How would the French approach this situation?", and follow their lead.

37

Adopt a Sense of Joie de Vivre

I t is take-two of our last night in Paris, so we once again make our way over to the grounds of the Louvre for what feels like a final victory round. As the sun sets and casts its golden light on the city, I find myself swooning yet again. The evening has a dreamlike quality to it. The air is electric, and you get the sense that everyone out walking these streets tonight feels it too. I overhear a young girl declare to her parents, "You know, Paris really is the most magical place on earth!" It seems the famously French sense of *joie de vivre* is contagious, and I've definitely been bitten with the bug!

I've encountered this *joie de vivre* on past visits to France as well. Nowhere was it on greater display than in the stands of le stade Orange Vélodrome, home to the Olympique de Marseille football team. I was left speechless by the performance put on by the team's passionate superfans. Their antics were actually more entertaining than the soccer game. To say they were an exuberant bunch is a huge understatement. (If we'd been in Canada, every single one of those fans would have been arrested!)

How can the rest of us invite more joy into our lives? How can we embrace a zest for life, and infuse each day with a sense of enthusiastic wonder? This, of course, is an age old question, and I'm not going to pretend I've been enlightened to the secret of happiness! I wrote my book, *Elevate the Everyday* with the intention of exploring how to sprinkle our daily lives with more magic and positivity. I think a lot of it comes down to feeling grateful for what you have, investing time in your passions, and not taking yourself too seriously!

While I love visiting and dreaming about France, the truth is, I have a great life here in Canada, with so much to be thankful for. What parts of *your* life bring you the most joy? Are you rushing through your days so quickly, that you miss the opportunity to stop and appreciate all the goodness around you? Perhaps this book will serve as a little reminder that you have so many wonderful people, places, activities and small pleasures to look forward to each day.

Making time for passion projects is a big one for me. I do most of my writing in the early hours of the morning (5 a.m.) to make sure I can fit it into my schedule. Knowing that my writing desk is waiting for me, I wake up feeling enthusiastic, energized and excited to dive into the pages of the book I'm working on. What are you most passionate about in life? What sorts of activities allow you to lose track of time? What is your definition of good old fashioned fun? Pull out a journal and actually take the time to create a top ten list. Are you carving out enough time to explore your passions, or do they sit at the very bottom of your list of priorities? It's time to bump them up to the top spot!

Life is too short to be serious all the time! Fill your days with more humor, whimsy and make-believe. I really enjoy sprinkling silly dashes of French fun throughout all aspects of my life. I named my male poodle Coco Chanel (Coco for short). He could care less that everyone thinks he's a girl, and truth be told, he really does act like a little princess. I like to pretend he is a stylish little Parisian *caniche*, strutting his stuff down the streets of Paris.

You are never too old to play pretend or indulge in a little daydreaming. What areas of your life could you create an atmosphere of whimsy? The next time you visit your local coffee shop, why not slip on some headphones and play a little French café music? Pretend that you are people watching on *boulevard St. Germain*, instead of the main street of your hometown. Pull out your journal and take note of how you feel and what you see. I do this sort of thing all the time! It's one of the techniques I use for writing, but it also allows me to mentally transport myself to all sorts of fabulous destinations.

Living life with a sense of *joie de vivre* is accessible to each and every one of us, French or not!

A Note from The Author

*M*erci beaucoup for joining me on this little getaway to Paris. I hope you enjoyed yourself as much as I did! In fact, I have to admit, while I wrote most of this book in a fast and furiously inspired state, I took my time to meander (or *flâne*) through the last few chapters. I really didn't want the book to end, because in a sense, the writing process allowed me to lose myself in the intoxicating magic of Paris for just a bit longer.

What I've come to realize, is that the spirit of Paris is accessible to each and every one of us, whether you've visited the City of Light in person, or only in your dreams. You can *choose* to live a French inspired life, no matter where you call home. Capturing the essence of Paris is really about inviting a sense of deliciousness into your everyday. It's about *choosing* to live a life that embraces beauty, wonder, mystique, lightheartedness, style, simplicity, romance, history, culture, art, connection, fabulous food, and a joyful attitude or *joie de vivre*. I hope my musings have sparked a sense of enthusiasm in you and have inspired you to carry a piece of Paris in your heart (and panties!) wherever you go.

If you enjoyed my writing, please check out some of my other books, which are all available on Amazon. They cover a wide range of lifestyle topics including personal style, beauty routines, household management, home décor, travel, fitness, personal finances, health, food, attitude…and so much more!

I also have a *petite* favor to ask. If you enjoyed this book, would you be so kind to take a moment and leave a review on Amazon? (Pretty please, *s'il vous plaît* and *merci beaucoup*) As a self-published author, reviews are incredibly valuable, helpful and greatly appreciated. They allow me to gain feedback on my writing, spread the word about my books, and connect with my wonderful readers!

The time has come for us to say *au revoir* and head our separate ways. I wish you a decadent, delicious and fabulously French inspired life—your very own version of *la vie en rose*. Bonne chance mes amies!

Gros bisous,

Jennifer

Other Books by Jennifer Melville

Elevate the Everyday:
Actions and Ideas to Enhance the Experience of Daily Life

Elevate Your Personal Style:
Inspiration for the Everyday Woman

Elevate Your Health:
Inspiration and Motivation to Embrace and Maintain a
Healthy Lifestyle

Elevate Your Life at Home:
Inspiring Ideas to Add Joy, Peace and Magic to Your Homelife

Preloved Chic:
Stylish Secrets to Elevate Your Wardrobe With
Second-Hand Fashion

Seashells in my Pocket:
50 Ways to Live a Beach Inspired Life

About the Author

*J*ennifer Melville is a self-published author. She decided to embark on a writing career because she wanted to tap into a community of like-minded individuals who share in her enthusiasm for living well and seeking ways to elevate daily life. She is a professional accountant by trade, who approaches life with an analytical and observant mind. Jennifer has been exploring the concept of elevating the everyday for over twenty years. She is passionate about family, health, fitness, fashion, nutrition, nature and all the beauty life has to offer.

Jennifer lives by the sea in beautiful Nova Scotia, Canada with her husband, two sons and little poodles Coco and Junior.

You can connect with her by email, on her blog, or on her Instagram page.

jenniferlynnmelville@gmail.com
www.theelevatedeveryday.com
www.instagram.com/the.elevated.everyday

Printed in Great Britain
by Amazon